Lionel Messi
Hard Work Makes A Star

2023 Noah Press © All Rights Reserved

All rights reserved. No part of this publication may be reproduced, distributed, or transmitted in any form or by any means, including photocopying, recording, or other electronic or mechanical methods, without the prior written permission of the publisher, except in the case of brief quotations embodied in critical reviews and certain other noncommercial uses permitted by copyright law.

This book is a biography. Information contained within this book is for educational purposes only. Although the author and publisher have made every effort to ensure that the information in this book was correct at press time, the author and publisher do not assume and hereby disclaim any liability to any party for any loss, damage, or disruption caused by errors or omissions, whether such errors or omissions result from negligence, accident, or any other cause.

TALK TO US
hello@noah-press.com

ON JUNE 24, 1987, A BOY WAS BORN IN ROSARIO, A BIG CITY BY A RIVER IN ARGENTINA.
NO ONE KNEW AT THE TIME, BUT THAT BOY WOULD GROW UP TO BE SOMEONE VERY SPECIAL INDEED.

AND EVERYONE IN THE MESSI HOUSEHOLD BONDED OVER ONE THING...
SOCCER!
THEY LOVED IT, THEY LOVED WATCHING IT AND THEY LOVED PLAYING IT.
MESSI PLAYED ALL DAY IN THE PARKS WITH HIS BROTHERS AND COUSINS.
WHEN HIS DAD FINISHED WORK, HE WOULD COME STRAIGHT HOME AND HELP HIS SON WITH SOCCER TIPS AND TRICKS.

AND WHEN HIS DAD WAS TOO BUSY, HIS GRANDMA STEPPED IN. IN FACT, SHE STARTED TO BECOME JUST AS COMMITTED TO HIS TRAINING AS MESSI WAS. SHE WOULD TAKE HIM TO MATCHES AND CHEER HIM ON FROM THE SIDELINES. SHE WAS HIS BIGGEST FAN!

BEFORE LONG, EVERYONE STARTED TO REALIZE THAT LITTLE MESSI WASN'T JUST HAVING FUN OUT THERE...
HE WAS GOOD.
SO GOOD, IN FACT, THAT HE JOINED HIS FAVORITE TEAM, NEWELL'S OLD BOYS, WHEN HE WAS JUST SIX-YEARS OLD.

AND IN SIX YEARS, HE SCORED OVER 500 GOALS FOR THEM! HE DAZZLED THE CROWDS ON THE FIELD, AND THEN PERFORMED TRICKS FOR THEM AT HALF-TIME.
FROM THE VERY BEGINNING, HE WAS A BORN SHOWMAN, FULL OF STYLE AND SKILL.

AT THIRTEEN, HE IMPRESSED THE SCOUTS AT BARCELONA SO MUCH THAT THEY SIGNED HIM IMMEDIATELY.
THIS WAS IT. HE HAD GOT HIS CHANCE TO PROVE JUST HOW GOOD HE REALLY WAS.
HE STRUGGLED AT FIRST.
HE HAD COMPLETED HIS GROWTH HORMONE THERAPY NOW, BUT HE WAS STILL SMALLER THAN EVERYONE ELSE. HE WAS SHY, TOO, AND DIDN'T SAY MUCH TO HIS TEAMMATES.
THE OTHER PLAYERS WEREN'T EVEN SURE THAT HE COULD TALK.

BARCELONA WEREN'T LETTING HIM PLAY MUCH IN THE YOUTH TEAM, EITHER. HE KNEW THAT IF HE GOT THE CHANCE TO SHOW EVERYONE WHAT HE COULD DO ON THE FIELD, THEN THEY WOULD SEE THAT HE WAS SPECIAL.
HE JUST HAD TO BE PATIENT.
SO EVEN WHEN ENGLISH TEAMS STARTED TO SHOW SOME INTEREST IN SIGNING HIM, HE REFUSED TO LEAVE BARCELONA.
THEY WERE THE TEAM THAT HAD BELIEVED IN HIM, AND HE WASN'T GOING TO LEAVE BEFORE HE HAD PROVEN HIMSELF.

AND THE MORE HE PLAYED, THE BETTER HE BECAME. HE WAS RUNNING RINGS AROUND HIS OPPONENTS IN THE YOUTH LEAGUE. SO MUCH SO THAT THE FIRST TEAM STARTED TO PAY ATTENTION. ESPECIALLY SOMEONE CALLED RONALDINHO.

THE LEGENDARY BRAZILIAN MIDFIELDER HAD TAKEN NOTICE OF THE YOUNG TRICKSTER DURING SOME TRAINING MATCHES, AND HE WAS IMPRESSED. WITH THIS KIND OF SUPPORT, MESSI FOUND HIMSELF RISING THROUGH THE RANKS PRETTY QUICKLY INDEED.

BUT MESSI DIDN'T REST.
IF ANYTHING, HE BEGAN TO WORK EVEN HARDER. HE WAS TRAINING EVERY DAY, GETTING STRONGER, BIGGER, MORE SKILLFUL. IT DIDN'T MATTER THAT HE WAS YOUNGER AND SMALLER. HE KNEW THAT IF HE WORKED HARD, HE WOULD BE UNSTOPPABLE.

THEN, WHEN MESSI TURNED EIGHTEEN, HIS DREAM BECAME A REALITY.
HE WAS PUT IN THE STARTING LINE-UP.
HE WAS NOW A KEY PART OF THE BARCELONA TEAM, AND HE HAD MORE THAN EARNED HIS PLACE THERE.

THE WORLD WAS FINALLY SEEING MESSI FOR WHO HE WAS.
A SOCCER PLAYER LIKE NO OTHER.
A KID FROM A FAMILY OF SOCCER-FANATICS, PLAYING FOR ONE OF THE BIGGEST TEAMS IN THE WORLD.
AND THEN... WELL, WHAT DIDN'T HE DO?

HE WON THE UEFA CHAMPIONS LEAGUE, THE UEFA SUPER CUP, THE FIFA CLUB WORLD CUP, LA LIGA, COPA DEL REY, THE COPA AMERICA AND EVEN THE FIFA WORLD CUP.
THERE WAS BARELY A TROPHY OUT THERE THAT MESSI DIDN'T WIN.

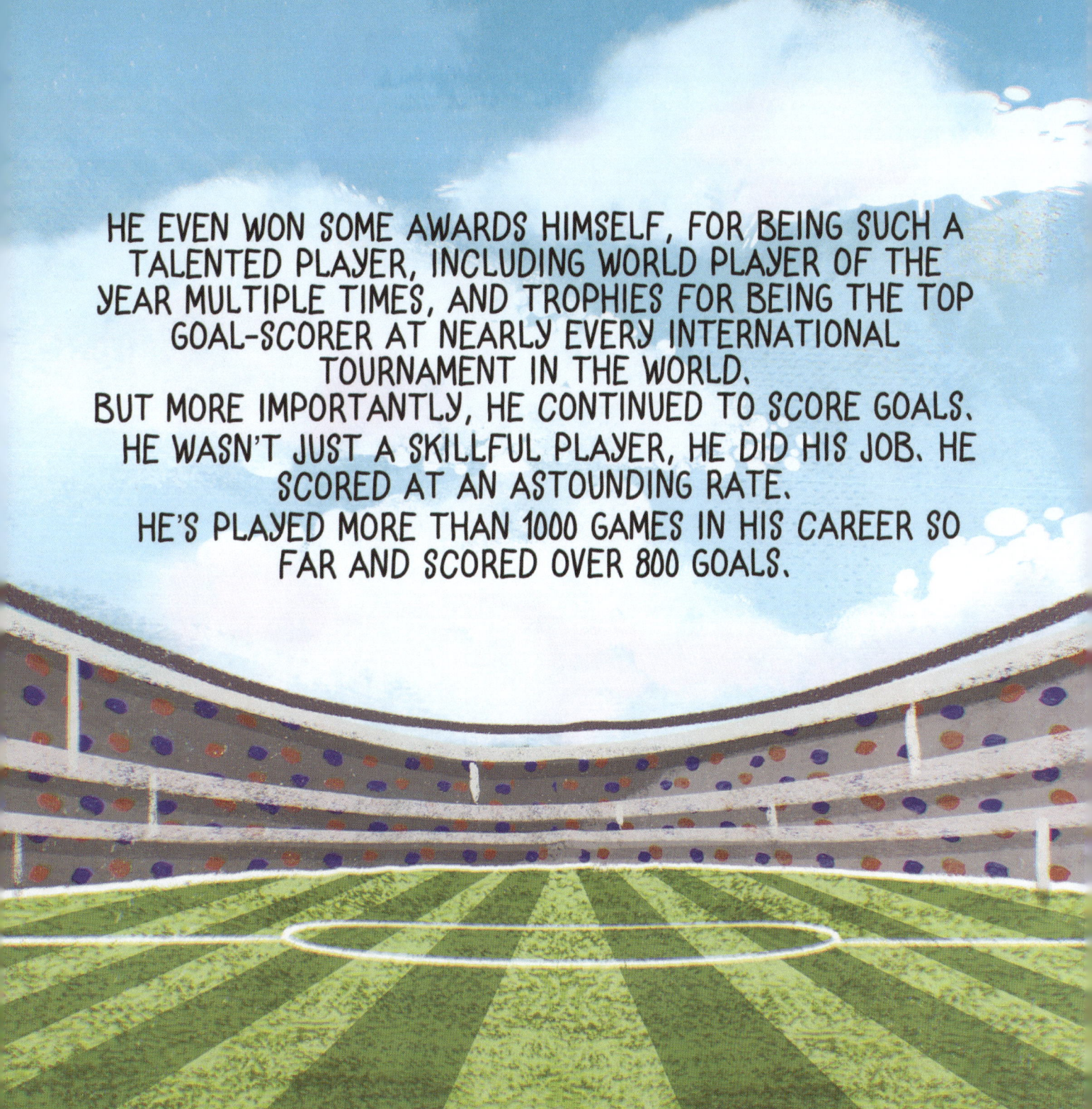

HE EVEN WON SOME AWARDS HIMSELF, FOR BEING SUCH A TALENTED PLAYER, INCLUDING WORLD PLAYER OF THE YEAR MULTIPLE TIMES, AND TROPHIES FOR BEING THE TOP GOAL-SCORER AT NEARLY EVERY INTERNATIONAL TOURNAMENT IN THE WORLD.
BUT MORE IMPORTANTLY, HE CONTINUED TO SCORE GOALS. HE WASN'T JUST A SKILLFUL PLAYER, HE DID HIS JOB. HE SCORED AT AN ASTOUNDING RATE.
HE'S PLAYED MORE THAN 1000 GAMES IN HIS CAREER SO FAR AND SCORED OVER 800 GOALS.

THERE'S NO DOUBT THAT LIONEL MESSI WILL GO DOWN AS ONE OF THE GREATEST PLAYERS EVER.
HE CONTINUES TO DAZZLE AND AMAZE WITH HIS CONTROL OF THE BALL, WHILE HE RUNS CIRCLES AROUND THE BEST DEFENDERS IN THE WORLD.
BUT GUESS WHAT?

HE'S NOT DONE YET.
MESSI KNOWS THAT AS LONG AS HE CONTINUES TO WORK HARD, TO PRACTICE AND TO DO WHAT HE LOVES, HE WILL KEEP SCORING GOALS. AND MORE IMPORTANTLY, HE WILL CONTINUE TO ENJOY PLAYING THE GREATEST GAME IN THE WORLD.
SO JUST LIKE MESSI, REMEMBER THAT ANYTHING IS POSSIBLE IF YOU BELIEVE IN YOURSELF AND DO YOUR BEST TO ACHIEVE IT. WHO KNOWS — MAYBE ONE DAY YOU'LL BE BECOME ONE OF THE WORLD'S GREATEST SOCCER PLAYERS.

Printed in Great Britain
by Amazon